Johnston-Hale
PUBLICATIONS

Somewhere
inbetween

Joanne Boyle

Illustrated by
Steffi Krenzek

Produced by
Johnston-Hale Publications
in the United Kingdom
2024

www.johnston-hale.co.uk

Issue 2

Author Joanne Boyle
Illustrator Steffi Krenzek

Johnston-Hale
PUBLICATIONS

The named contributors of this book have asserted their rights under the Copyright, Designs and Patents Act of 1988 to be identified as the authors and illustrators of this work.

A note from the Poet

After the success of my poem 'Queen' which went viral, I went on to write a selection of poetry books about various things. 'Somewhere In Between' has been inspired by loss and feelings of empathy.

I hope, more than anything, that the poems in this book bring some comfort to the people who read them.

Thank you,
Joanne
xx

The Illustrator

My name is Steffi Krenzek, and I am an artist who paints and draws with a creative spirit and a left-handed flourish, straight from the heart of Germany, Europe. My journey on this planet began in 1974 and I have been painting from the earliest days of my childhood.

In addition to my paintings, I am an illustrator for children's books. My artwork often weaves a tale with poetry, bringing words and visuals together in a harmony that speaks to the soul. A new book with the great poet Joanne Boyle is a collaboration I'm really proud of.

In my belief, every monumental accomplishment has its roots in something incredibly small and pure. This might be the reason why painting children holds a special place in my heart. They embody the essence of purity and hope, with an innate belief in love.

You can find my work at:

steffikrenzek@instagram

https://m.facebook.com/steffi.krenzek

https://artsartistsartwork.com/vendor/krenzek/

https://www.etsy.com/de/shop/Fregenius

Dedicated to
My Mam
Joyce

Always a Lady

x

Somewhere inbetween

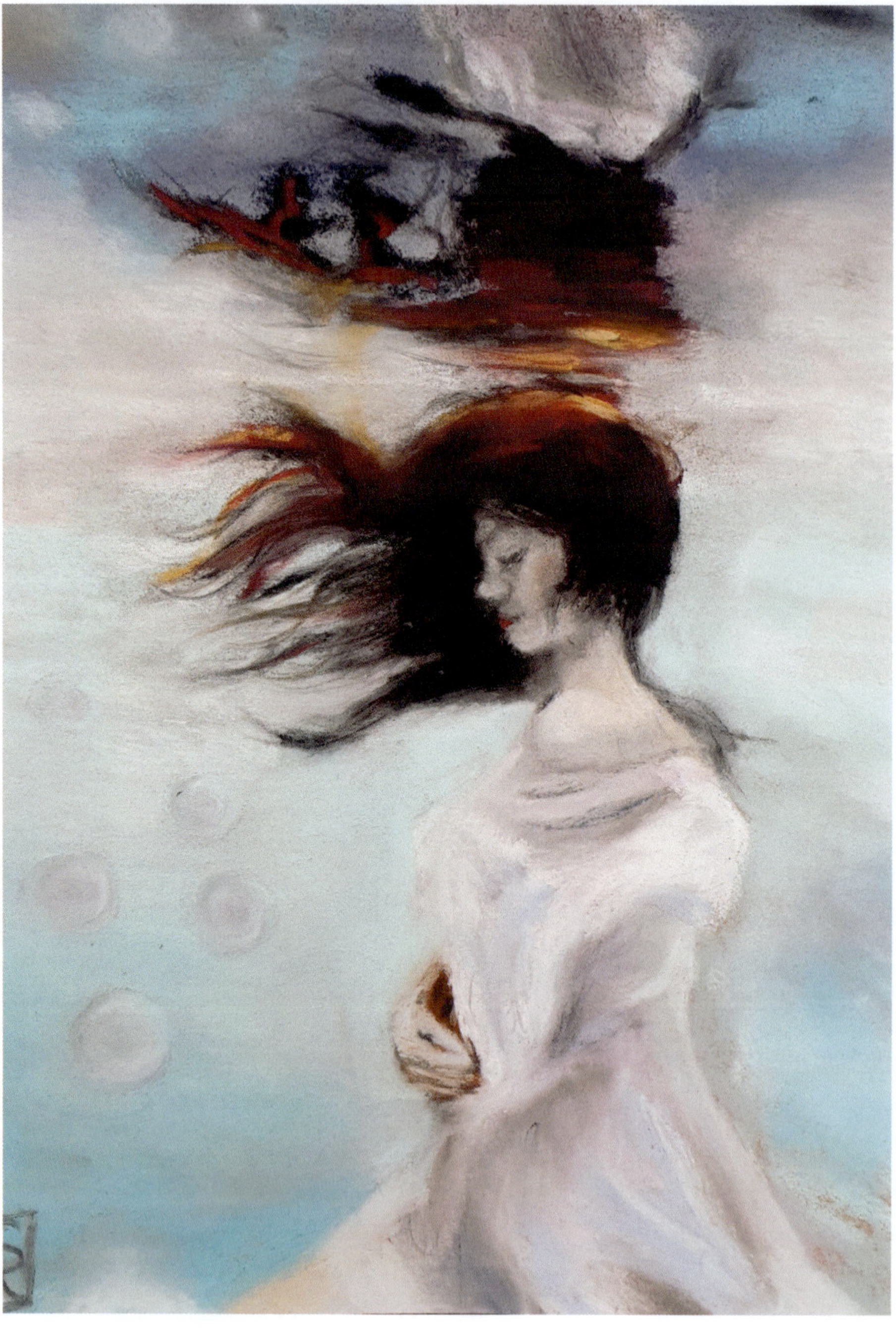

Somewhere In Between

I heard my mama calling. I haven't seen her for so long.
My Papa shouts my name from the cloud he sits upon.

In the distance I saw Grandma, holding Grandpa's hand.
They hadn't changed, as they stood there, hand in hand.

I could feel my body floating, as if I was in a dream,
yet I could hear sobbing. I was somewhere in between.

The angels were getting closer. The cries hurt my ears.
I felt a sense of warmth. I was wet from fallen tears.

Someone held my hand, in fact someone held each one,
but still I kept on rising whilst they kept holding on.

I could hear so many voices, just echoes in my head,
and as Mama called, I heard voices from my bed.

Not sure if I was dreaming or where I was meant to be,
I longed to see my Mama, but I now had a family.

I floated in between, torn with grief and love,
but as I opened my eyes, I had lost the one above.

Purpose

Without a purpose, there is no light to our day,
no warmth from a blanket or a place to stay.
The wind doesn't blow or whisper a name.
Nothing ever differs, as it's always the same.

Without a purpose, there is no pain to feel,
no sunny days or laughter to steal.
The raindrops that fall from way up high
land on your face, yet you remain dry.

Without a purpose, a dream is lost in space
and a social gathering is an empty place.
A blossoming flower may as well be dead.
The world holds nothing but pure dread.

Without a purpose, you will never know joy,
and disregard memories like an old broken toy.
Love is a word that you heard someone else say
and hope is used by those who pray.

Find your purpose and you will find you
and the light of day will then shine through.
You will feel the love run through your veins
and memories will stick like old tea stains.

Man Club

We laugh and have a pint, talk football or play pool,
making jokes of others, laughing at the fool.

Thinking silent thoughts, yet never daring to ask
when we have misunderstood the meaning of a task.

Laughing with the lads and knowing in your heart
you have got a friend who has been there from the start.

When the demons overtake and get behind your eyes,
dancing with the devil. No longer in disguise.

You open your darkest secrets and others follow too,
all the things you buried, thinking folk would laugh at you.

Someone cracks a joke; you break out in a smile.
A hope then peers through as there's been none for a while.

You look around the room and you now see past today.
You know you are still alive as your heartbeat begins to play.

Sometimes men think being a man means being strong,
but like a woman and kitchen sink those days are long gone.

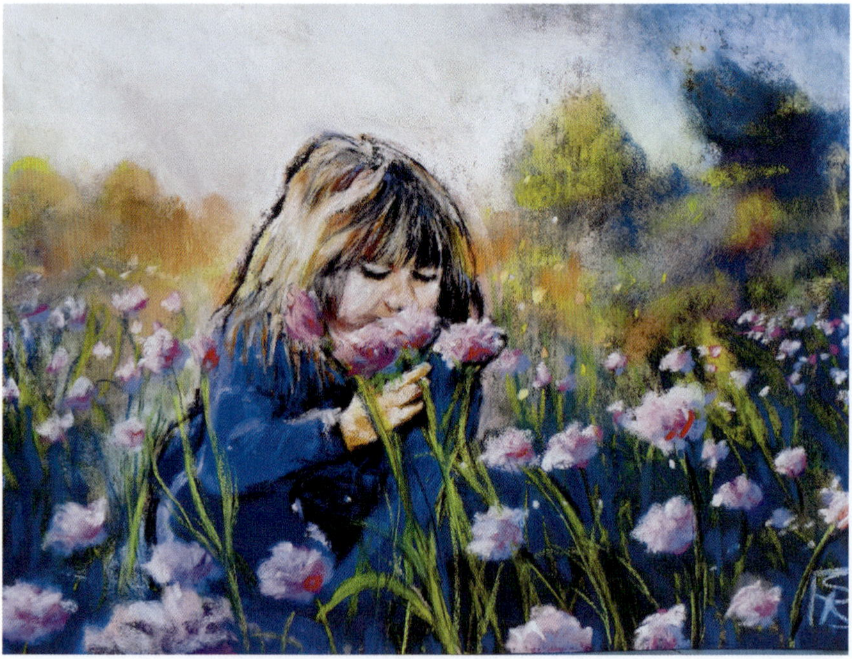

Amidst a Field of Flowers

Amidst a field of flowers, I sat and smelt just one.
I knew by the way it stood and how each petal shone,
I would choose this as the one I'd send to you,
the one I'd wrap with love and all my kisses too.

So, I picked it from a field from the ground it grew
and I held it in my hands as I carried it to you.
I got down on both knees and, as I bowed my head,
I wished you a happy birthday through the tears I shed.

I then placed the flower down; I put it on your chest.
I know you clutched it tightly from your place of rest.
I closed my eyes and pictured a memory from before,
and I found you in a memory and I smiled once more.

I got up from my knees and once again stood tall,
and as I looked around me, there was no one at all.
Just me and you in a moment, like we used to be,
in between two worlds sharing a memory.

The Warm and the Cold

I sit here tonight with the thoughts in my head,
of children in poverty with a floor for a bed.
My hands are cold and my feet are numb.
I think of the folk who don't have a room.

I take out a blanket and I want to give it away.
I wish for a home where all could stay.
The man in the doorway, the mother with no heat,
the hungry child with no shoes on their feet.

The innocent and the poor, the ones who inflict,
those who seek shelter from somewhere derelict.
I put on my dressing gown and hang my head low
as I look at my fire and its warm orange glow.

My bed is their dream and my dream is their wish.
I pray for all children to have food in their dish.
A cupcake to us is a gateau to others.
One slice of bread between a family of brothers.

The young and the old, The future and the past,
Soup and a blanket, A first and a last,
I climb into bed, warmed by a quilt.
I pray for the poor with a heart full of guilt.
I whisper, "Goodnight," in a puff of fresh air.
I am lucky to be here whilst others are there.

The Waiting Room

I tried calling you today. I will try tomorrow too.
I have tried so many times and still I can't get through.
I walk about in circles. This torment never ends.
I am just wanting advice, an appointment to attend.

I promise I won't bite you or keep for you too long.
I am just scared about my welfare. Is that wrong?
There is something going on, or I wouldn't make a fuss,
but I feel it is important and I have something to discuss.

A week has passed me by and I finally get through.
In my heart I feel some hope, soon short-lived by you.
You don't see me; I'm diagnosed through a phone.
What if my pain was caused through a broken bone?

I won't ring anymore. I bet you are pleased with that.
Staring at an empty chair, opposite to where you're sat.
Will you remember when my name is in the deaths? The
answer will be, "No," whilst my family are bereft.

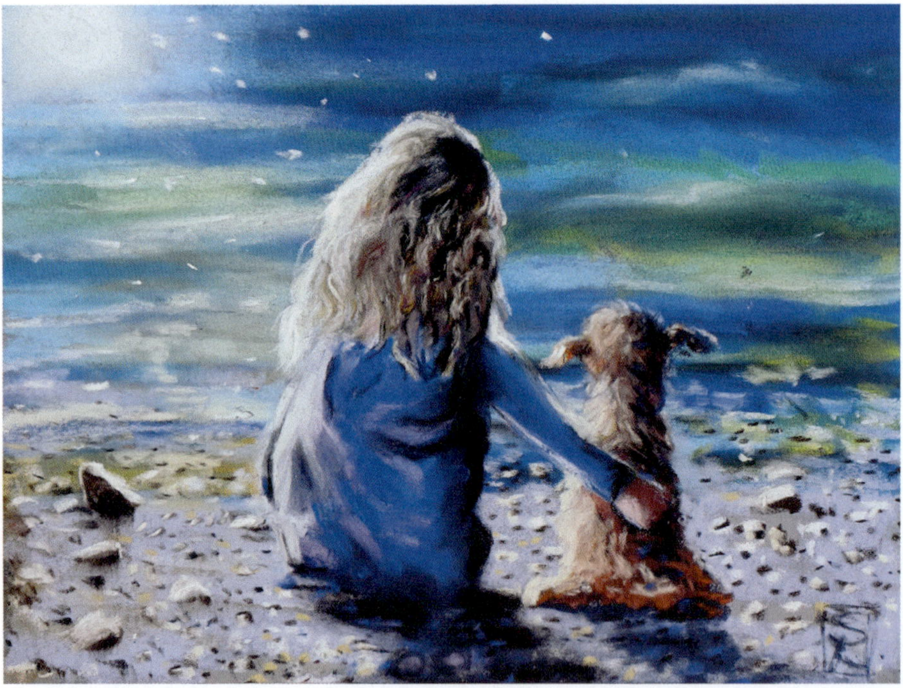

The Ears
That Cannot Speak

We shared so many secrets. I would listen and you'd tell.
I would lift my paw to yours if you weren't feeling well.

I would lay beside your feet, so you knew that I was near
I would make my presence known when I sensed fear.

I would bring my favourite toy, begging you to play.
I tried for you to focus so your mind didn't stray.

I had noticed on our walks your step lost its bounce
and when you threw my ball, I also lost my pounce.

Still, we remained best friends, your words into my ears
and the tongue I used so often to lick away your tears.

Then one day I waited but I knew you were gone,
and I had all the answers but a voice I had none.

It is then that I stopped listening as my ears fell,
and my barking wasn't heard as I tried to tell.

Today I Bought a Life

Today I bought a life with a few kind words I spoke.
I looked inside a soul and saw that it was broke.

I got my paintbrush out and put a smile on my face.
It is the first thing that we feel to help us to embrace.

I shouted out, "Hello," and how I hoped you are well.
You answered with a grumble but I soon got you to tell.

I listened with my silence. I gave you both of my ears.
Eventually you trusted me enough to share your fears.

I took you for a coffee, though my time was not my own,
but yours was being lengthened by the care I'd shown.

Your family wouldn't get that call to rip them apart
because you opened up to a kind and caring heart.

Kindness can't be bought in from a window display,
and time is bought from love and the only price to pay.

The Last Dress

They speak with sad hearts. I sense their building tears.
They talk of what you'll wear with pride above all fears.

They plan your party with detail, knowing it's your last.
Reminisce for the obituary as they recollect the past.

Your choice of jewellery is easy as it was your choice.
They had listened to your wishes when you had a voice.

They speak of the great mother who was loved so much.
This party is your last and that's why it means so much.

They shall dance their final dance holding you in the air,
slowly walking to the rhythm like no one else is there.

When the music stops and they lay you down to rest.
The tune of the final dance shall be a memory blessed.

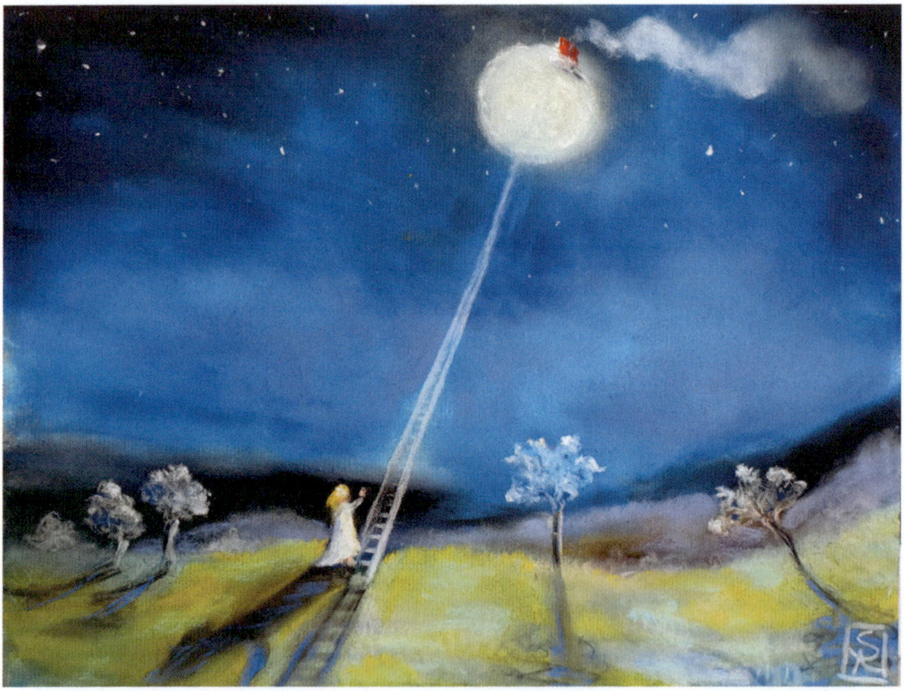

If Heaven Had a Ladder

I wrap my arms around emptiness.
I fill the space with tears.
I run to heaven in my mind,
telling God about my fears.

I tell him when you arrive,
he needs to send you back.
The world was not ready to lose you.
You had taken the wrong track.

I would lock the pearly gate
and safely store the key.
I would show you an army of love
that would be yours for eternity.

I would use all my strength to fight you,
to make you turn around.
I would put you on my back
and carry you down to the ground.

I guess that is why there are no ladders
that lead us to the sky,
because no one would be in heaven
as love wouldn't let them die.

Traffic

I have never understood, since you went away,
how traffic keeps on moving and night still turns to day.

How the wind keeps on blowing leaves on the ground.
How the clocks keep ticking when you're not around.

How people go to work or are shopping with friends,
picking clothes to suit them and setting off new trends.

Social media is still working; still used by everyone.
How come no one notices? Do they know you're gone?

Sitting at a bus stop; the bus is running late.
Time still moving forward but I'm stuck in a date.

People stood chatting everywhere you look.
Yet I'm still on the page of the day that you were took.

The minutes turn to hours, the days into weeks,
yet my face is always wet from the tears on my cheeks.

I will never understand how the world moves on, when
mine has been stood still since you have been gone.

Not Today

You tell me you love me. I can hear what you say,
but I don't really care, at least not today.

I saw you wipe your eyes, tears caused by me,
yet my emotions don't stir with anything I see.

You keep supplying me food, drinks for my thirst,
but I am so full of emptiness I feel I could burst.

I go into my room, a place I should know,
but still. I am alone no matter where it is I go.

An unfamiliar world, yet a one I've met before.
A ground that burns my feet, but I don't feel the sore.

My phone keeps on ringing; someone says, "Hello,"
checking I am still here but today I will not go.

Every moment is different, yet the dark is never light.
You keep telling me I am strong and I need to fight.

Your words fall on deaf ears so silently I say,
"I am not going anywhere, at least not today."

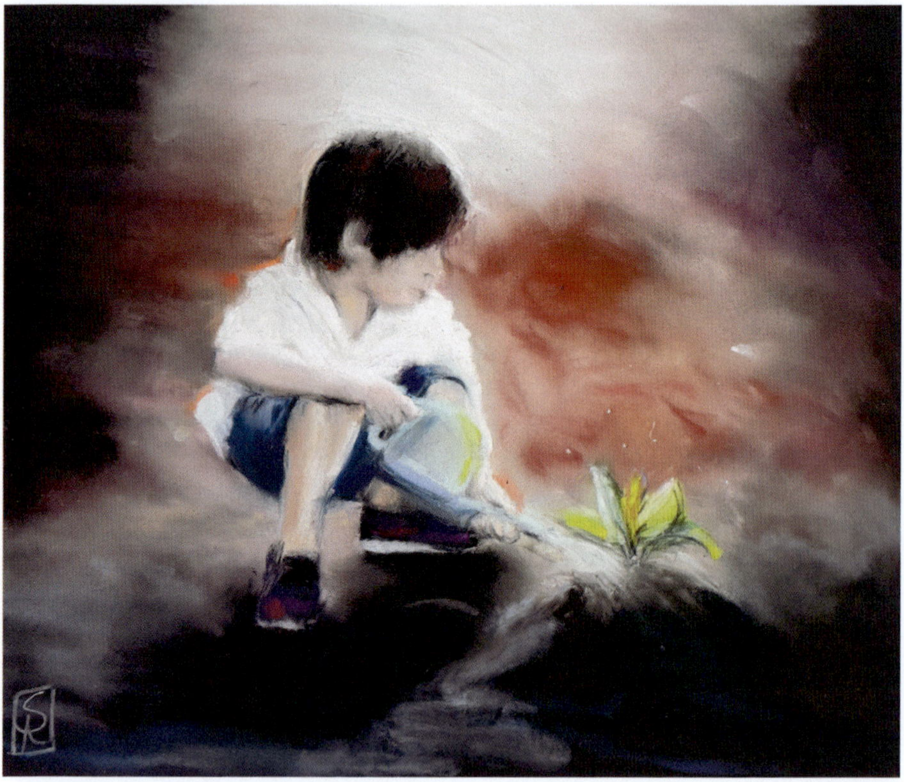

I Picked You a Flower

I picked you a flower, Nana, to say what I can't say.
I find it difficult to feel overwhelmed in such a way.

I picked you a flower, Nana and when I see your smile,
I didn't know what to do but I knew it was worthwhile.

I find feelings very confusing. I don't understand.
Emotions overpower me and then you take my hand.

You look me in the eyes and though I try to pull away,
you don't let me go and I find I want to stay.

I get all muddled up at times but I keep on loving you.
So, I picked you a flower, Nana to remind you that I do.

The Empty Hole

I woke up from my sleep this morning,
which I didn't want to do.

My days are nothing but nightmares now
and I don't want to make it through.

I pour myself a coffee
as I look out to the sky.

The cup now fills with tears;
The coffee cup never runs dry.

I go back in my mind
and relive the times we shared.

I try to fill this empty hole
by grasping memories spared.

The hole cannot be filled though,
and I don't know how to live.

Tomorrow shall be the same
as I have nothing more to give.

I search everywhere for answers,
knowing there's none to find.

I long to close my eyes again,
to put darkness to my mind.

I walk the streets of ignorance.
My loss is there unknown.

I look upon their children
as I mourn the loss of my own.

I must go on living though,
with this great big empty hole.

It represents my love for you
when my heart was stole.

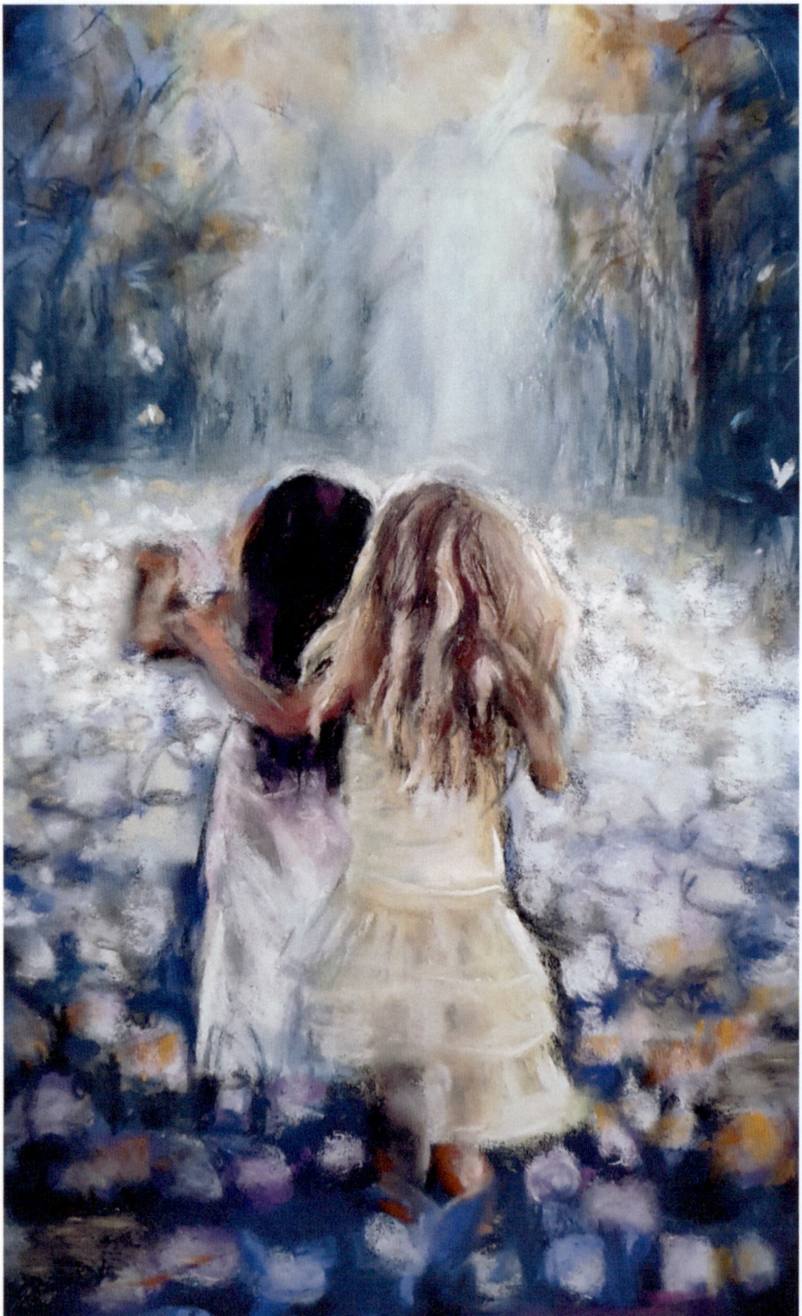

An Angel Tapped me on my Shoulder

An angel tapped me on my shoulder and said,
"Can you come with me?"
I felt a warm sensation as I stepped from my body.

I then felt a drop of rain as she took my hand.
The rain then poured faster and I didn't understand.

I was told that they were tears falling from your heart,
that you now felt it was broken due to my depart.

It was then I looked back and saw you standing there.
I whispered in your ear as I stroked your hair.

Whenever you need me just go inside your mind.
I will meet you in a memory, the sweetest one you find.

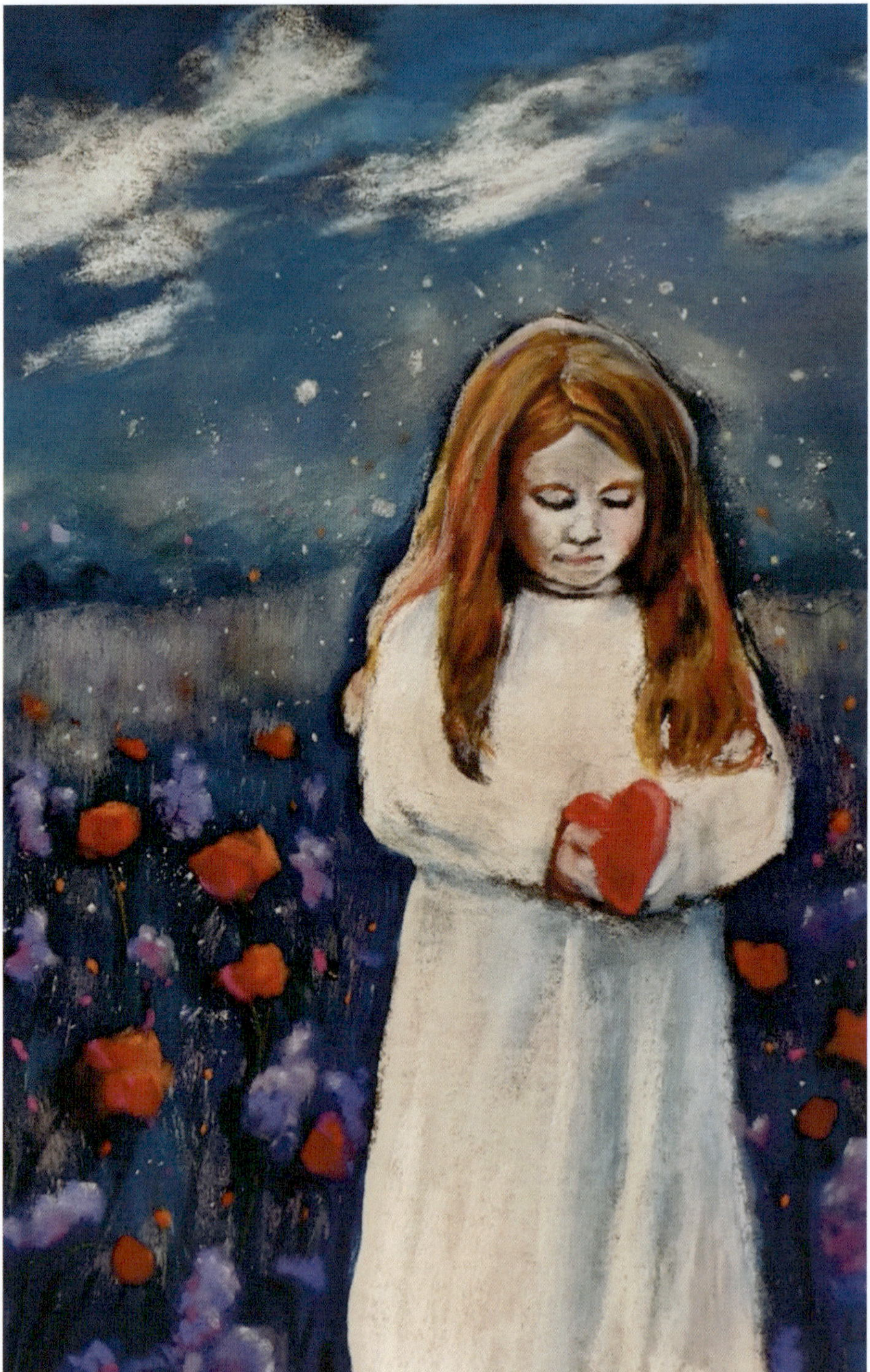

My Beating Heart

I looked for you in memories, like I was told to do.
I searched through hazy clouds and couldn't find you.

I thought it was due to the rain so I closed my eyes
to stop the rain from falling and hope the wetness dries.

I went back to the times we would sit and have a chat.
I couldn't find you there. I wondered where you were at.

I then closed my eyes less tightly and felt the rain eased.
I found the fog cleared, the less my eyes were squeezed.

I was now in a field of love and the sun began to shine.
I found a beating heart and realised it was mine.

I picked it up and held it but only for a while.
I knew I had to put it back for me to share a smile.

I felt it was still beating slightly in my hand.
I looked up to the sky as I whispered, "I understand."

My heart is where you are. You took it when you went
but leaving me without you was never your intent.

I will Meet you there

On the days I miss you most I'll close my eyes and sleep.
I will meet you in my dreams in a moment we can keep.

I will greet you with a hug and with things I want to say.
I will meet you under the sun, a different place each day.

I will meet you by the river or back at our old home, and
at times I cannot find you, in my dreams I will still roam.

I will meet you in a coffee shop at your favourite place.
I don't care just where it is as long as I see your face.

I will meet you at a park so you can watch children play.
You can take their laughter to heaven to hear every day.

I will meet you on each birthday we no longer share.
I don't care where it is but I will meet you there.

I will meet you in the sunshine or in the pouring rain.
I will walk through any storm just to see you again.

I will meet you in my thoughts a million times a day,
along with every memory I am lucky I can replay.

In case I Forget

If the day comes and in case I forget,
remind me always of the baby I met.
Sit by my side and tell me a story,
One of our lives; one of glory.

In case I forget that I watched you grow,
I am telling you how I loved you so.
Remind me of times from happier days.
Keep me alive in the sunshine's rays.

In case I forget all the memories we made,
the fun and the laughter and games we played,
keep showing me the album, the one in your heart,
reminding me always at each day's new start.

In case I forget the love that we built,
the stories we would tell from under our quilt,
know that I had so much love in my life;
as a mum and a nana and a happy wife.

In case I forget my grandchildren's faces,
remind me of us and familiar places.
In case I forget then I am glad you have not,
and you will cherish the memories that I have forgot.

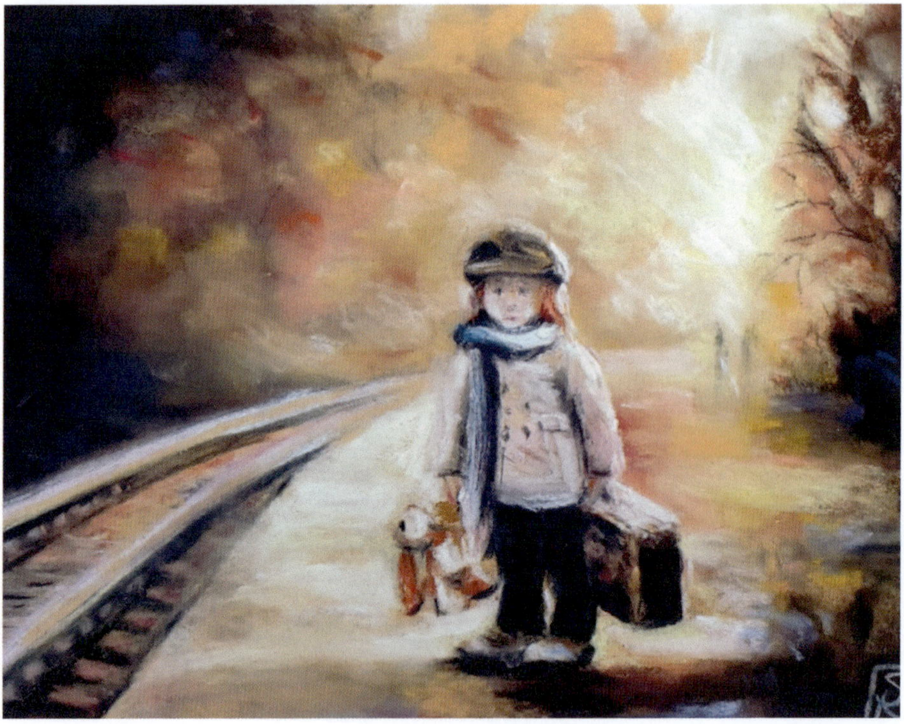

The Station

Patiently I waited to board the train of life.
I hoped to meet my parents, a father and his wife.

I knew I'd take a journey and meet friends on the way and
some would leave the train and others want to stay.

I'd visit different places and memories would be made.
Leaving will bring me regret and wishing I had stayed.

Others will bring me sorrow and I'll be glad to leave.
All the time I will be aging and my youth I won't retrieve.

I don't know where I am going or who will go or stay.
I am sure there will be lessons to be learnt on the way.

My family will get off when they don't like what I do.
Sometimes they will get back at the next station or two.

A view from each window, portrayed from how I feel,
learning to decipher who is fake and who is real.

My train is pulling up now and I am about to board.
I will look forward to the memories that I will record.

My Child

There was a time in my life I couldn't imagine you here.
Now I couldn't face a day without having you near.

When you were first born and I held you close to me
I made a promise to my heart that I'd keep for eternity.

I'd sit and count my pounds to see what I could afford,
the smile if I could treat you being my ultimate reward.

I would put you in my bed because of fears in my mind.
I was always showing love and teaching you to be kind.

I knew one day you'd be older and I'd have to let go. You'd
become one of two and our family would grow.

I guess I never knew I had so much love to give and
that the grandchildren would be another reason to live.

Yesterday you were my baby that I carried at the start.
You outgrew my arms but can never outgrow my heart.

A mother and her daughter or a father and a son,
all tied up with enough love to be shared by everyone.

Sleep

I close my eyes to find you. I know that you are there.
You are like particles of dust that are irritating my glare.

You dance with my thoughts; I try to keep them still
by emptying my mind but the thoughts just refill.

I can feel your heavy load packed behind my eyelids
but I can't lessen your burden as lack of sleep forbids.

It feels like it's awakened by every tick and tock.
And everywhere I look there is another clock.

I try to count the sheep as they approach the fence
but I find my thoughts wander and it makes no sense.

I know that I am lucid, yet in a land of in between.
I long to reach the place where I can go and dream.

Eventually this dust that is scratching at my eyes
will dissolve into the sleep and so I'll have my prize.

Then night will turn to day and I won't function at all
and I will spend my day longing for nighttime to fall.

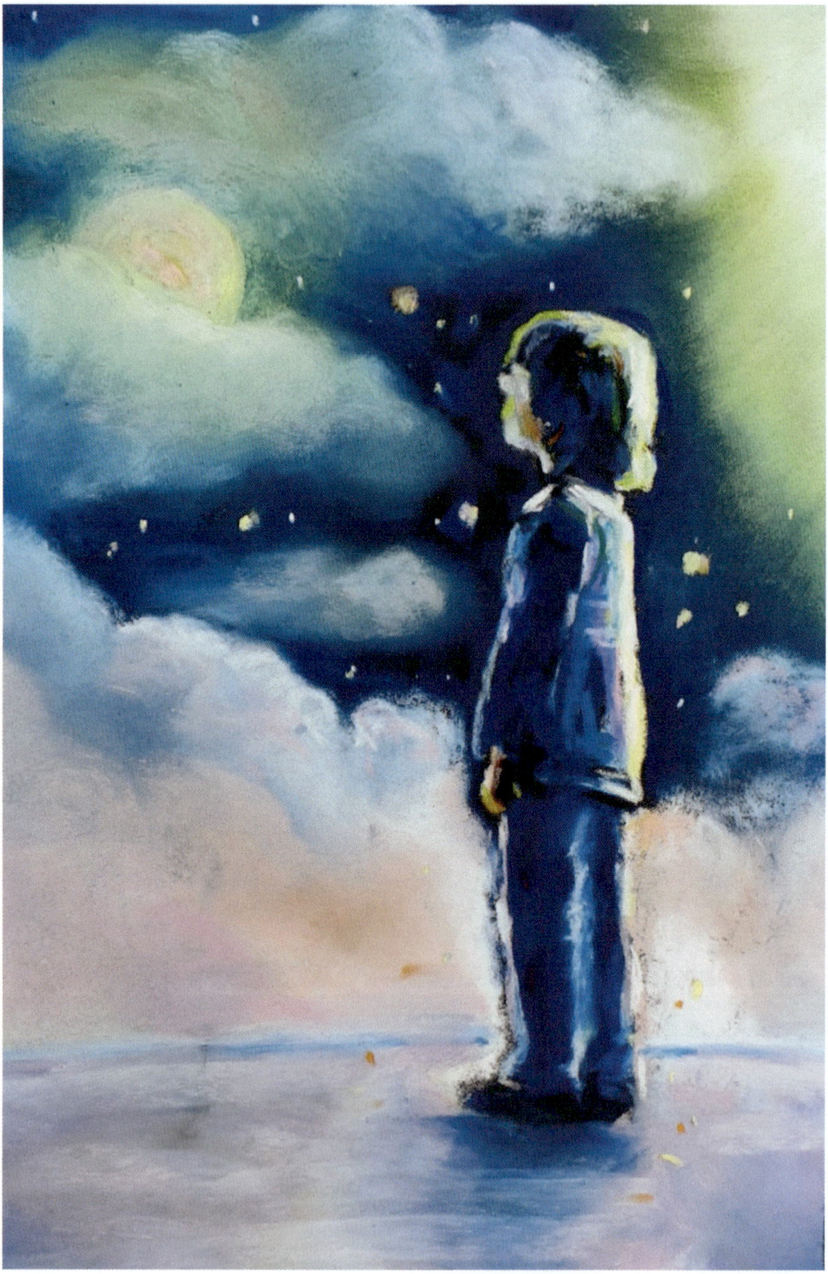

A Wonderful World

All alone with his thoughts, his dreams and his fears.
His world overcome by the noise in his ears.

The touch of a cloth, unfamiliar to his skin.
A battle of emotions felt from within.

An anxious feeling with his twiddling thumb.
The sound of music is like a beating drum.

A crowd of people takes his breathe away.
A routine is needed every day.

The smell of cut grass or of yeast in his bread
is enough to set fireworks off in his head.

The colour of his food or the way it is cut
can send a signal of turmoil straight to his gut.

The most loveable boy in a world of his own,
teaching others around him about the unknown.

Without

Without bad we wouldn't know good.
Without can't there wouldn't be could.
Without the rich there'd be no poor.
Without temptation we wouldn't have lure.

Without getting hurt we wouldn't know love.
Without below there wouldn't be above.
Without sacrifice there'd be no gain.
Without emotion we wouldn't know pain.

Without hello there'd be no goodbye.
Without life then we wouldn't die.
Without evil there'd be no kind.
Without loss we wouldn't have find.

Without food then we wouldn't eat.
Without houses there'd be no street.
Without sadness there'd be no sorrow.
Without today we wouldn't have tomorrow.

Without yesterday there'd be no today.
Without leaving we would not stay.
Without you there'd be no me.
Without forever, no eternity.

Without You

I try not to think about where I would be
without you in my life being there for me.

You gave me a home with a rooftop to share.
Without you in my life would I even care?

You gave me my friend, the best I have had.
Without you I would crumble each time I'm sad.

You taught me that silence is a peaceful place.
Without you I'd be living in a lonely head space.

You don't pass judgement when I do wrong.
Without you I don't believe I'd be this strong.

You smile when I'm happy and your eyes light up.
Without you I'd have a half empty cup.

You love for me to spend time with others around.
No need for jealousy as no insecurities found.

You taught me the meaning behind true love.
With you I am home and you are my other glove.

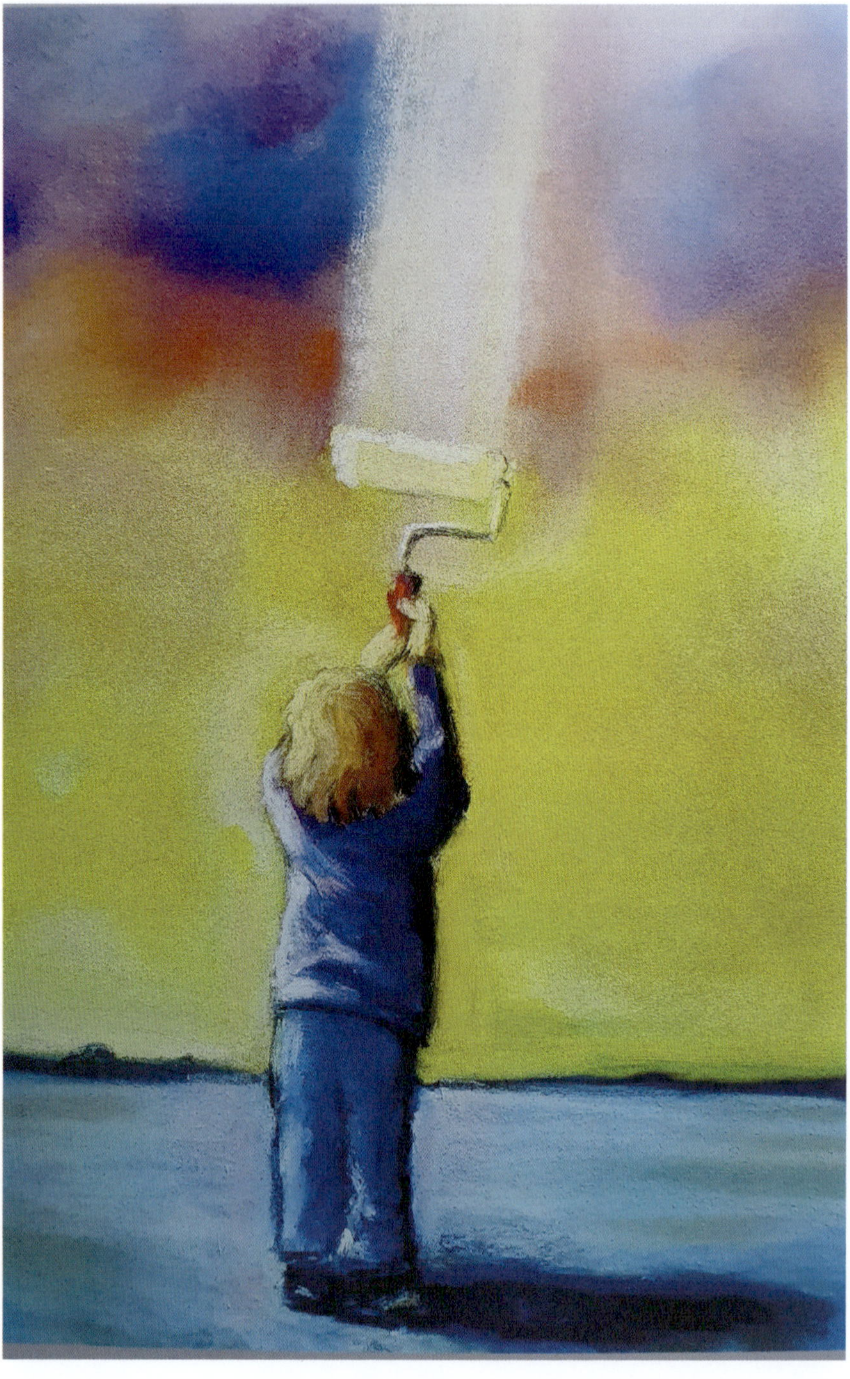

A Colourful World

"Can we play a game, Mammy, the one we always play,
the one with the same actions and words as yesterday?
Will you put Teen Titans on whilst I eat my tea
and make sure my chicken nuggets are cut equally?

When was World War Two? Is that a blossom tree?
When did the Titanic sink? How long will Daddy be?

I don't want to go to the party. I'll stay home with you.
I'll follow you to the kitchen and to the bathroom too.
Can we go to the park now? Is it time to go?
I am sorry I keep asking but I really want to know.

When was World War Two? Is that a blossom tree?
When did the Titanic sink? How long will Daddy be?

Are my chicken nuggets ready? Oh no they are not right.
Will you put Teen Titans on? When will it be night?
Can you hear a lawn mower? What's that awful smell?
Can we play that game again, the one I like so well?

When was World War Two? Is that a blossom tree?
When did the Titanic sink? How long will Daddy be?

Two worlds brought together through innocent eyes.
Autism and its colours on a painting that never dries.

Remembrance

"God, do you mind if I ask you a question?"
"No not at all my son. What is on your mind?"
"How come I am in heaven
when fighting isn't kind?"

God smiled at me just then,
as he knelt to my height and,
with a movement of his hand,
he turned day into night.

The world was now in darkness,
with an old familiar smell.
I then recognised the ground,
the exact place that I fell.

I wondered why God showed me this,
so, I asked him why?
He said it was my answer
as to why I'm in the sky.

Then night turned back to day
and, through a parted cloud,
God told me to look
and to take notice of the crowd.

"Do you see all those people?
They are there because of you.
Your heart remained pure.
You did what you had to do."

I looked through the parted clouds
at a world that had stood still.
I asked why no one was moving.
God said that, "They will."

He told me of a silence,
A tribute for all to remember.
It happened on the 11th hour
on the 11th day of November.

God then closed the clouds, and
as he turned and looked at me,
he saw a tear in my eye and
he passed me a hankie.

"Why do you cry my precious boy?
You are a hero that has not been forgot."
"And this is why I cry, Father,
because I now see that I am not."

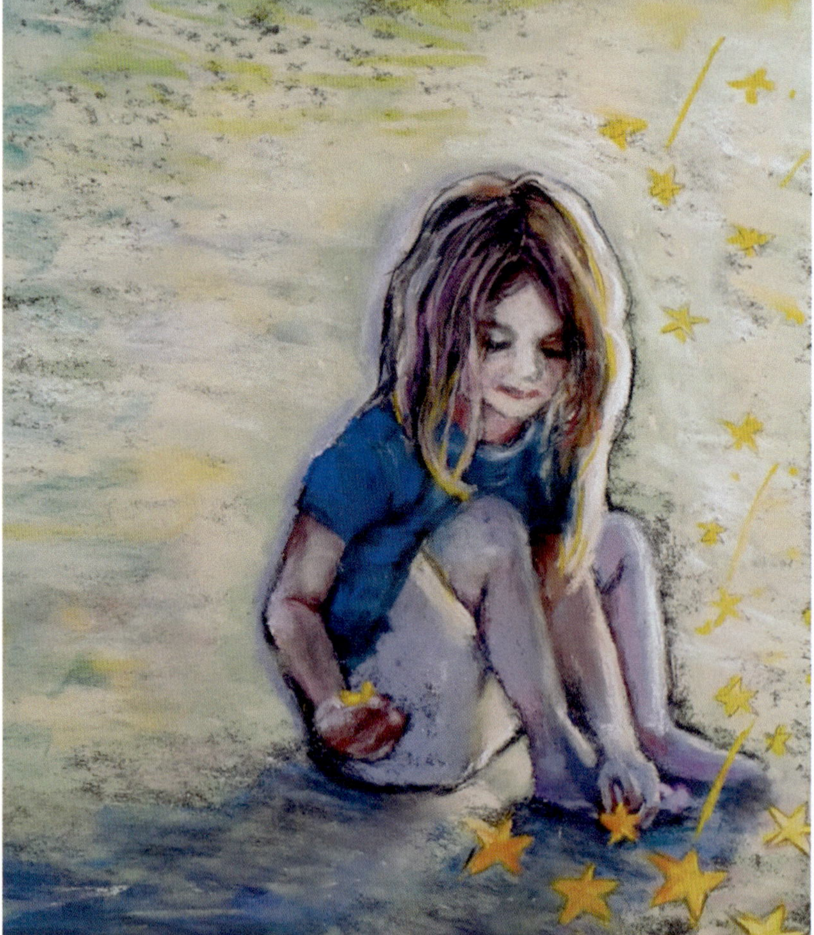

Collecting Moments

Today I collected happiness and put it in my pocket.
I then collected hope and put it in my locket.

I then chose a moment for a blessing
that I could pass on to another,
a gift of ever after to a daughter from her mother.

I picked a time for forgiveness
in case it's something that I need.
I held on to generosity to overcome my own greed.

I planted future moments like seeds that will grow.
I'll dig them out if ever bitterness decides to grow.

I'll give a moment to my friend,
in the hope it will help her to remember
who she used to be before that illness in November.

I'll wrap some up in love and give them as a gift,
to be unwrapped at any time that spirits need a lift.

I'll give moments to my family,
enough for them to measure.
The value of our memories is a priceless treasure.

The Stork

When I was chosen to be born and asked to pick a family
I asked God to show me the ones who would get me.
He opened the clouds and people were everywhere,
but only you stood out, so I said, "Please put me there."

God knew I had a gift that not all would understand.
He knew I would get frustrated and need a helping hand.
He said that I wouldn't see the world that others see, then
he leaned and whispered, "You have a speciality."

He told me not to be afraid of the magic I would find.
He said I was unique, just one of a certain kind.
He told me there'd be things I wouldn't comprehend.
He said that if I broke then you would help me mend.

I couldn't wait to meet you. I now see what he meant.
We have had so many years of precious moments spent.
You have entered my world knowing I can't enter yours.
You have loved me for myself, not noticing any flaws.

My words are very limited but I love you very much.
The hand that you both hold is the hand I love to touch.
When the stork came for me, he said I'd get a new name.
I'd no longer be called autistic for not being the same.

Waves of Life

We are going on a journey. It is called the Waves of Life,
so, buckle up and be prepared for challenges are rife.

Waves will wash over you. You will think you may drown.
Your clothes won't dry out and this will slow you down.

Still, you'll keep on surfing, in and out, up and under.
Some days you'll love the waves and others you'll wonder.

Some days you'll surf smoothly and all will be still.
Enjoy these precious moments and use them to refill.

When you see dry land ahead then go and take a rest.
Welcome the laughter from the folk you like the best.

You will have waves of sorrow when someone goes away.
These waves will keep on coming; accept that it's okay.

Let them surf beside you as you make new memories.
Appreciate the warming sun and the whispering breeze.

Let the waves of life soak you in all that they give.
Let each wave be a part of the life you live.

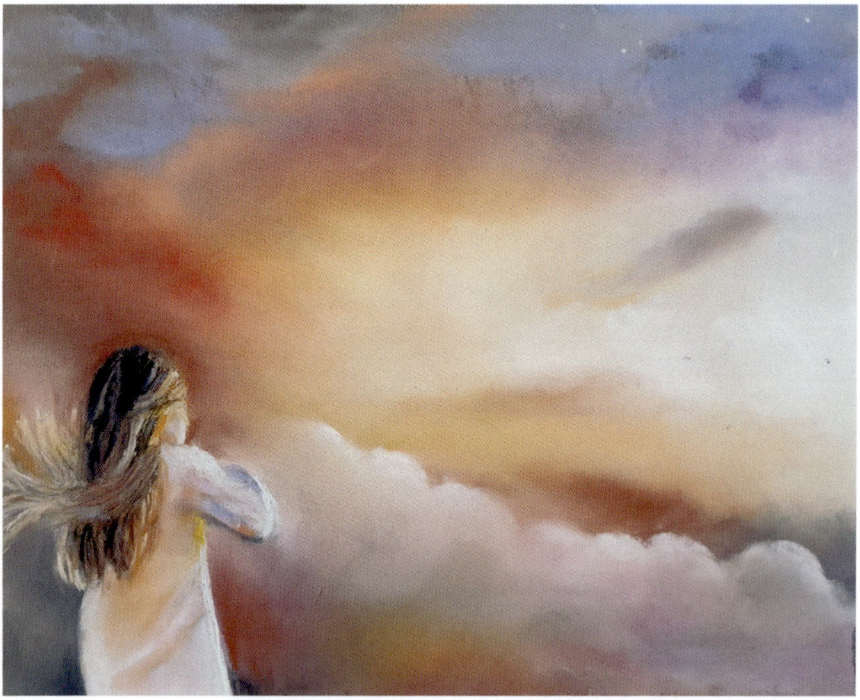

Before you go Mamma

Before you go, Mamma, and leave this world behind,
take with you our memories; there are lots to find.

Before you go, Mamma let me hold you once more,
I don't want to forget when you walk through heaven's door.

Before you go, Mamma, smell the scent I wear.
Take a piece of me with you, so you will know I'm there.

Before you go, Mamma, let me put a tissue in your pocket
to remind you of my tears and the hair in your locket.

Before you go, Mamma, will you look into my eyes?
So you won't forget the colour, the same as the skies.

Before you go, Mamma, will you promise me this,
that you will return every night to place a little kiss?

Before you go, Mamma, let me wrap you in my love.
Keep it with you always as you move to the world above.

Goodbye Mamma, until we meet again.
Now go toward the light and free yourself from pain.

A Letter to Cancer

I can't bring myself to write the word 'dear' on this paper
so, I'll start my letter asking why you want to break her?

I'm finding it hard to remember a time before we met.
Yet the time you introduced yourself is one I can't forget.

I never thought I'd be the person I am since meeting you,
a person that can smile whilst hating everything you do.

I go deep inside my mind and sit opposite you in a chair.
I ask you many questions but the answers aren't there.

What makes you creep inside my skin and of others too?
You care nothing for your victims. It is all about YOU!

Sometimes the pain is very bad but what hurts me more
is seeing someone I truly love crumbling on the floor.

I may feel physical pain that your evil likes to spread
but the torture to my family is why my tears are shed.

The treatment gives us hope that you will disappear
but I know the seed you planted will always leave me fear.

I'll keep on writing you letters, though you won't reply
but along with everyone else, I will pray for you to die.

The Fatal News

I heard that fatal news today as you stood beside my bed.
Although I had prepared myself for all the things you said,
I could feel myself going numb; I wanted you to go away.
I wanted the life I knew. I wanted yesterday.

Still, you stood there screeching, scratching at my brain,
running over my ever after with the wheels of your train.
I'm not sure if you saw me cry, or did I wait for you to go?
I tried to cover my ears because I didn't want to know.

Although I heard your words, I just didn't comprehend,
so I played my childhood game, the one where I pretend.
I thought a thousand thoughts. I wondered what I'd done.
I looked towards the door; maybe I could run.

And then I thought of you, my children of the earth
and, instead of facing death, I saw what I was worth.
I wasn't afraid of going, as much as leaving you behind.
Who would be there to listen to what was on your mind?

Then I realised I would still as I'd be everywhere.
Every decision that you make, I would still be there.
It is then I found my peace with the life I got to own.
Cancer will not defeat me …. The illness I will DISOWN.

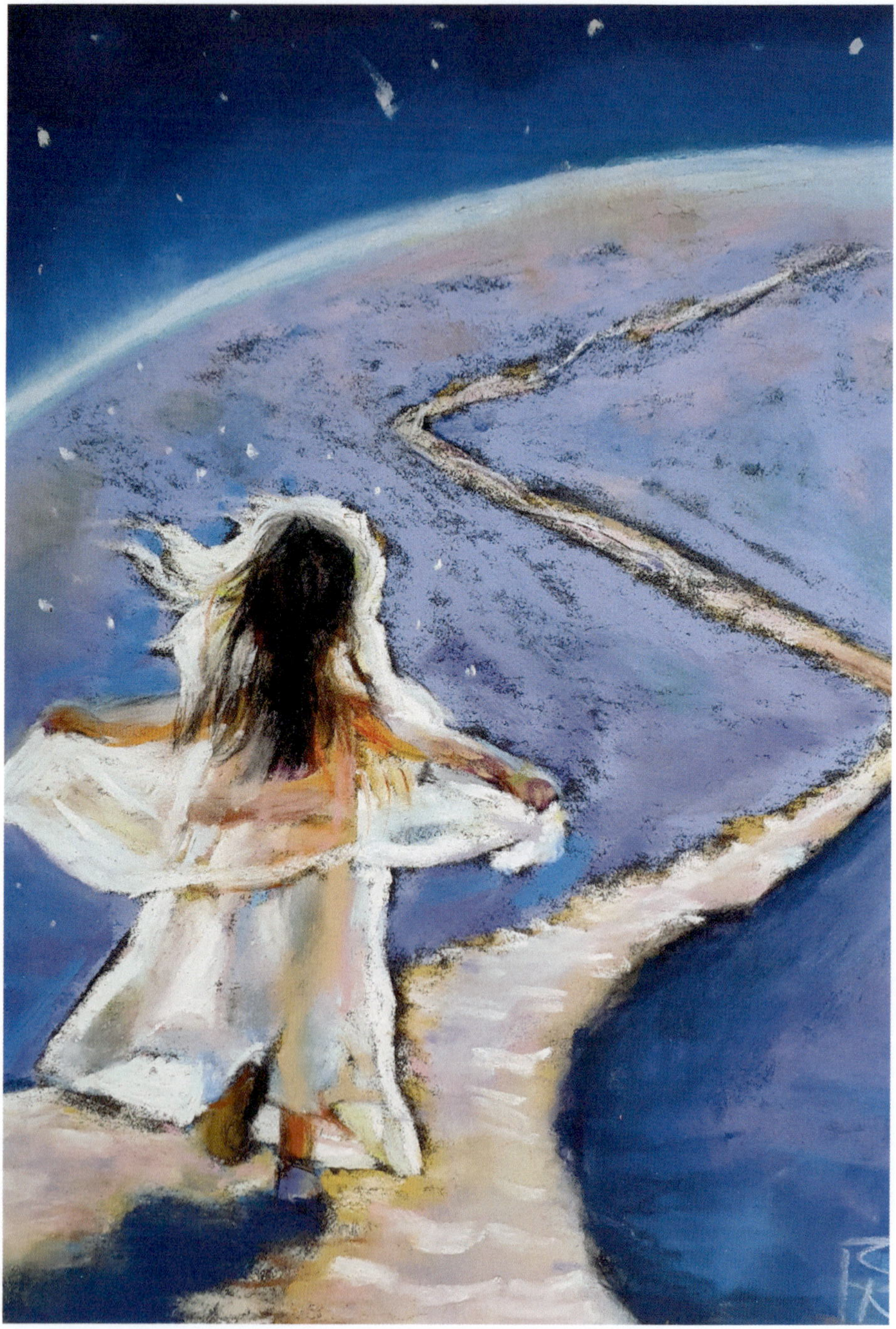

The Journey

At first, I left my words, though yours were not unheard,
then I left my sight but my vision was not blurred.

Then I left my body, though you still held my hand.
I kissed you on the forehead through a knotted strand.

I looked around the room, as though I wasn't there,
Then I felt myself rising through a mist of air.

I thought I heard you cry but it became a distant noise.
I tried to catch your eye as I fought to hold my poise.

Then I was amidst the clouds, so breathtaking and blue.
I was going on a journey, heading to somewhere new.

I headed toward a stairway; at the bottom was a gatemade from
shiny pearls and I looked forward to my fate.

As I walked up every stair, stars began to shine.
I soon reached an archway that led to a light sublime.

An angel came to greet me, I swear I knew his face.
He opened his kingdom and said I'd earned my place.

My journey was complete but I never took my heart.
I left that there with you so we would never be apart.

Another World

It's like looking at another world,
a one where you live,
a world that I can't reach
but a one I try to give.
Your eyes are full of dreams,
ones I hope to reach.
Your thoughts are so unique,
so much I hope you teach.

The colour of your food,
the texture and the shape
makes me ask if your world
is where other foods escape.
When repetitive questions
are met with answers the same,
it never stops you asking,
the same one again.

The same show is on tv,
but each time it's something new,
and although I know the words,
I don't tire of watching you.
We meet somewhere in the middle,
your world and mine.
A parent in the spectrum and
her child with its own design.

Mother Earth

Once upon a time, the earth was just soil.
Nothing ever grew and there was nothing to spoil.
Along came a theory, each to their own,
but suddenly a flower had grown.
From one little petal a seed did fall
and flowers blossomed, both big and small.
They filled the land that we named Earth
and from each seed was another birth.
Trees became forests and pathways merged.
Roads were formed and swamps were purged.
Along came man, or an ape to some.
Nevertheless, he created Mum.
A house was built and named a home,
be it built from straw or made from stone.
Food was caught from a stick or a spear,
whatever ran or swam in a river.
People learnt to create with their hands.
Unspoken words ruled the lands.
Life evolved in one way or another
and the soil of the Earth became known as Mother.
She gave us life that we passed on.
We discovered music from birds in song.
From a horse and cart and a water well,
a scrubbing brush and a service bell.
A dirty pinafore to a pretty dress,
hair tied back to disguise its mess.
From then till now she still gives birth
and carries the title of Mother Earth.

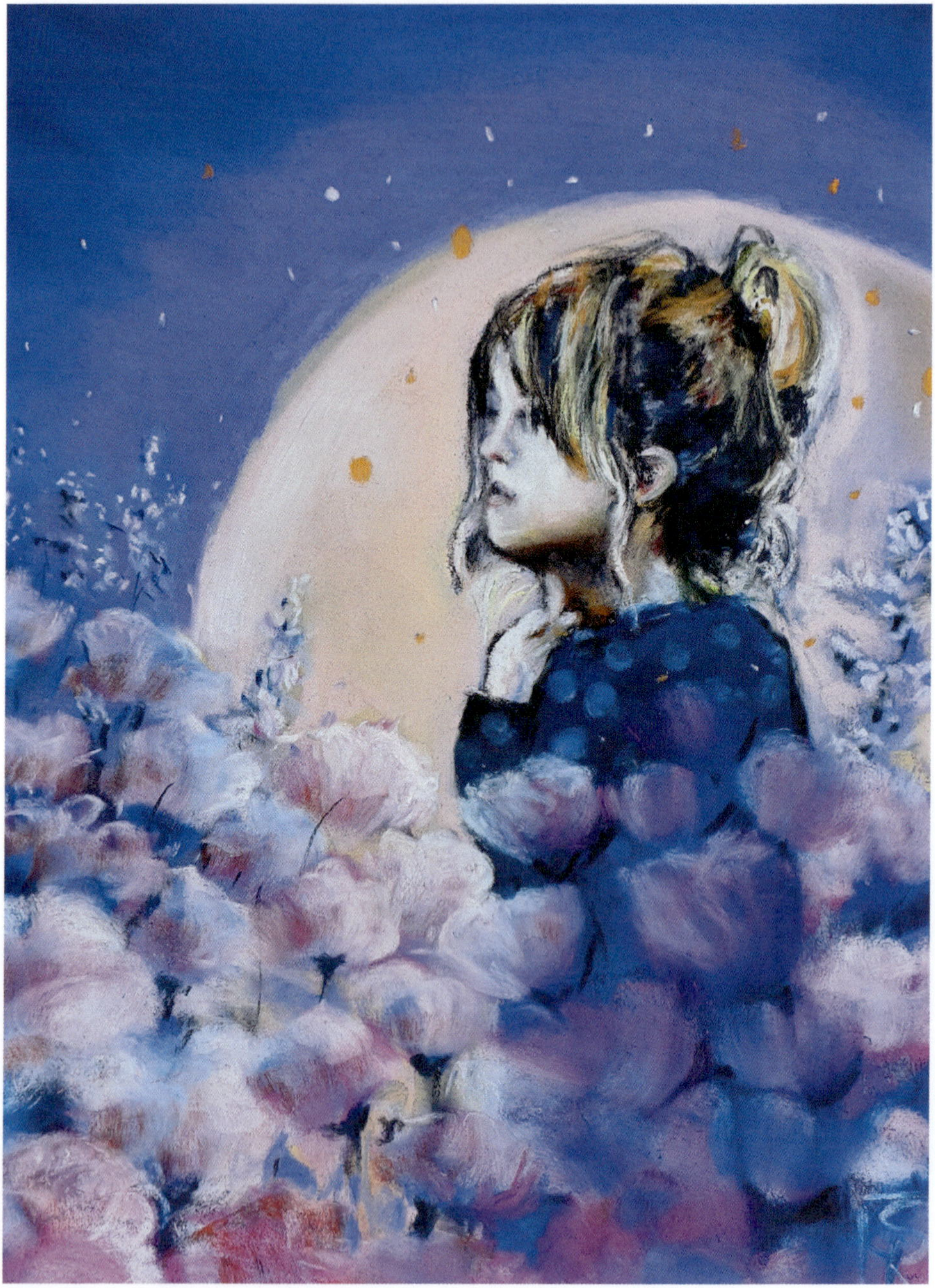

The Pass

God came to me today with an angel by his side.
He said it had been a while since my body had died.

He opened some clouds and said, "Look down there."
I saw so many memories floating everywhere.

Each memory shared found its way into my heart,
transported me to earth like we'd never been apart.

I went around in circles, visiting you all once more.
Heaven is a miraculous place with a forever open door.

I saw some of you sat crying and, as I dried your eyes,
I sent you a happy memory to use as a disguise.

I lingered around the laughter like a breeze in the air.
I am sure you were aware of my presence being there.

Time has gone so quickly but my memory still lives on.
I live in many moments. I am the lyrics in a song.

I am always watching you from my home in the sky,
still dancing in the memories you have of you and I.

PTSD Awareness

I thought when I left the chair,
that had tied me up in chains,
the nightmare I'd been living was yesterday's remains.
Then, as I was sitting peacefully
and someone came into the room,
I jumped up from my chair, back to a world of doom.
I cowered in the corner
with my arms wrapped round my chest,
my heart racing to escape but those demons knew best.
I felt a hand upon my shoulder
and I eventually heard a voice.
It was telling me to breathe, as if I had a choice.
I didn't want to look
for fear of who I'd see.
Was I in a memory or was this reality?
I didn't understand it all.
I was in a world of in between.
Lost in a mind of darkness, yet now a light did gleam.
That was the first of many,
where I'd transition to the past and
though each time was scary, I knew they wouldn't last.
With understanding ears,
I was told this had a name, and
that I was not alone, as PTSD is not a game.

The Fields of Paradise

I stroll through the fields of paradise.
I smell every flower I pass.
I breathe in the rustling tree
as I lay down on the grass.

I look at the sky above me.
I hear it calling my name.
I am not ready to leave this garden yet,
even though the good Lord came.

Down here I still feel life
although it is no more.
I am invisible to myself
but not ready for heaven's door.

I feel the ground beneath me,
though my shadow does not exist.
I am one of life's lost souls
with my name on a missing list.

I walk around in circles.
I long to see you again
but I know why you don't visit,
as it's like revisiting pain.

This paradise is my haven
and until my body is found,
I shall walk within its magic
and forget I'm not around.

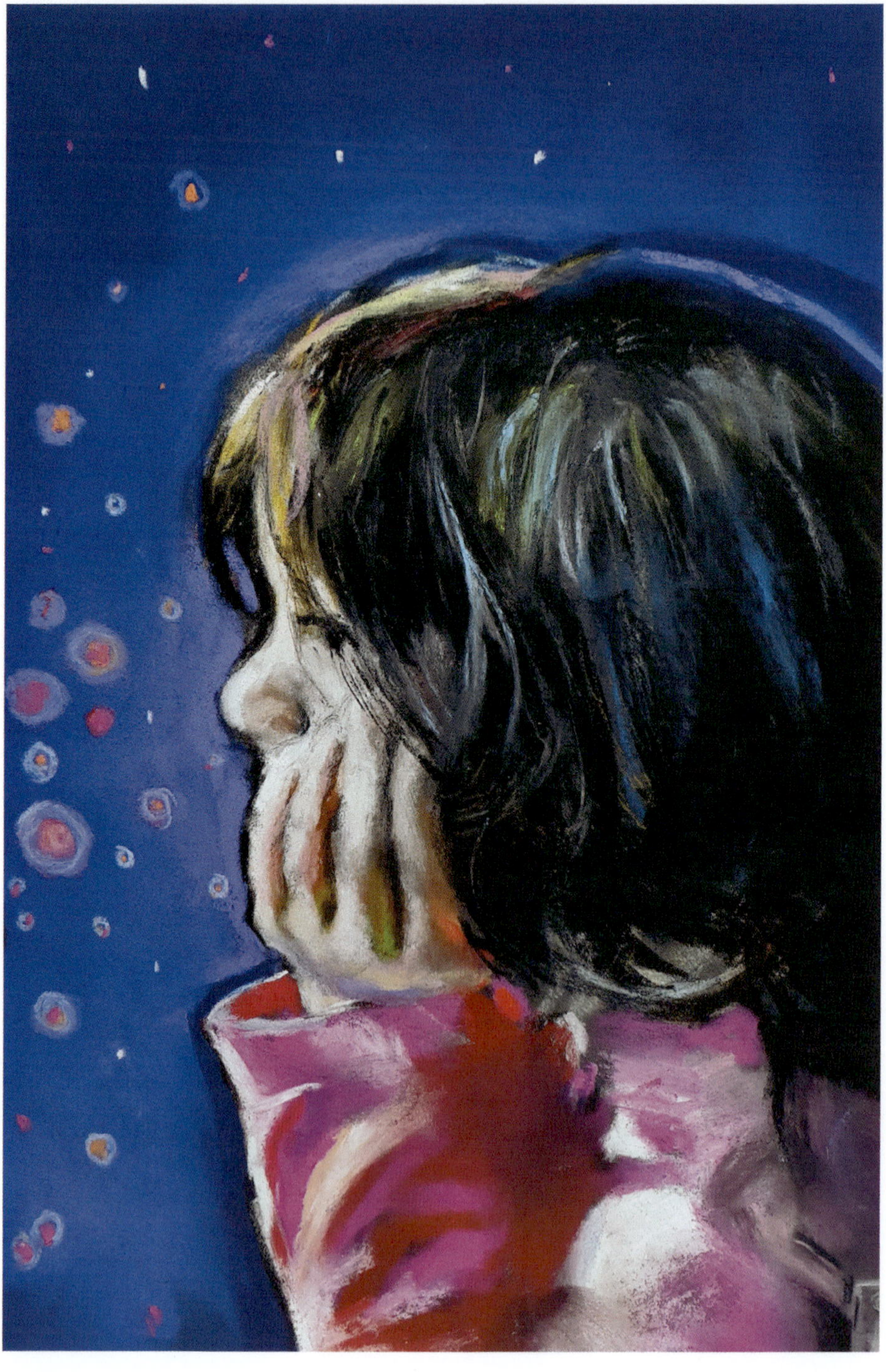

Words

I waved from the nursery door.
I stood in my usual place.
Mummy and Daddy waved back,
a smile upon their face.

I couldn't wait to tell them about Chloe,
the new friend that I'd met,
or about the pencil drawing
or the plaster mould I'd set.

I ran through the nursery door;
my hug is what they heard.
They asked how my day had been
but they never understood a word.

I could tell by the way they looked,
from each other then back to me.
They never gave the right answer
when I told them about Chloe.

I gave them my pencil drawing.
I told them it was a dog and a cat.
They said they could see it was Daddy
wearing a suit and a hat.

Why couldn't they understand me?
To me it was perfectly clear.
Maybe I spoke too quietly
so, I tried to shout in their ear.

They now think I am being angry
but I am just wanting to be understood.
I heard them say this is awful
and how they wished they could.

They worry about when I am older
and that others won't want to play.
They are fighting to get me help
so. when they ask, "How was your day?"

I will be able to tell them about Chloe,
though by then I may have forgot.
I hope more awareness is raised
because right now there isn't a lot.

Emptiness

You came back for me and took me wherever you went,
leaving a shell of non-existence in a world I now resent.

My laughter dances with yours as it echoes in the air.
My vision of a future without you is no longer there.

I walk with this empty hole that only you can fill.
I no longer look for memories. Time has now stood still.

My feet keep walking forward. My batteries have no life.
Everywhere is numb. I wouldn't feel the cut of a knife.

I search for you in my dreams to feel alive again, but
I keep living in the nightmare, too numb to feel the pain.

An existence without motive. A life without hope.
Eyes without a vision, emotionless enough to cope.

Tomorrow

Don't walk into tomorrow
with what you fear today.
Don't let yesterday's emotions
take the present ones away.

Don't dwell on past mistakes
or hope for tomorrow's dreams.
Just enjoy each moment's ripple
step over negative streams.

Don't open your morning eyes
with your nighttime vision.
Don't waste your time longing
for tomorrow's mission.

Don't think about what's gone,
or even what's to come.
Just enjoy living in the moment
and watch who you become.

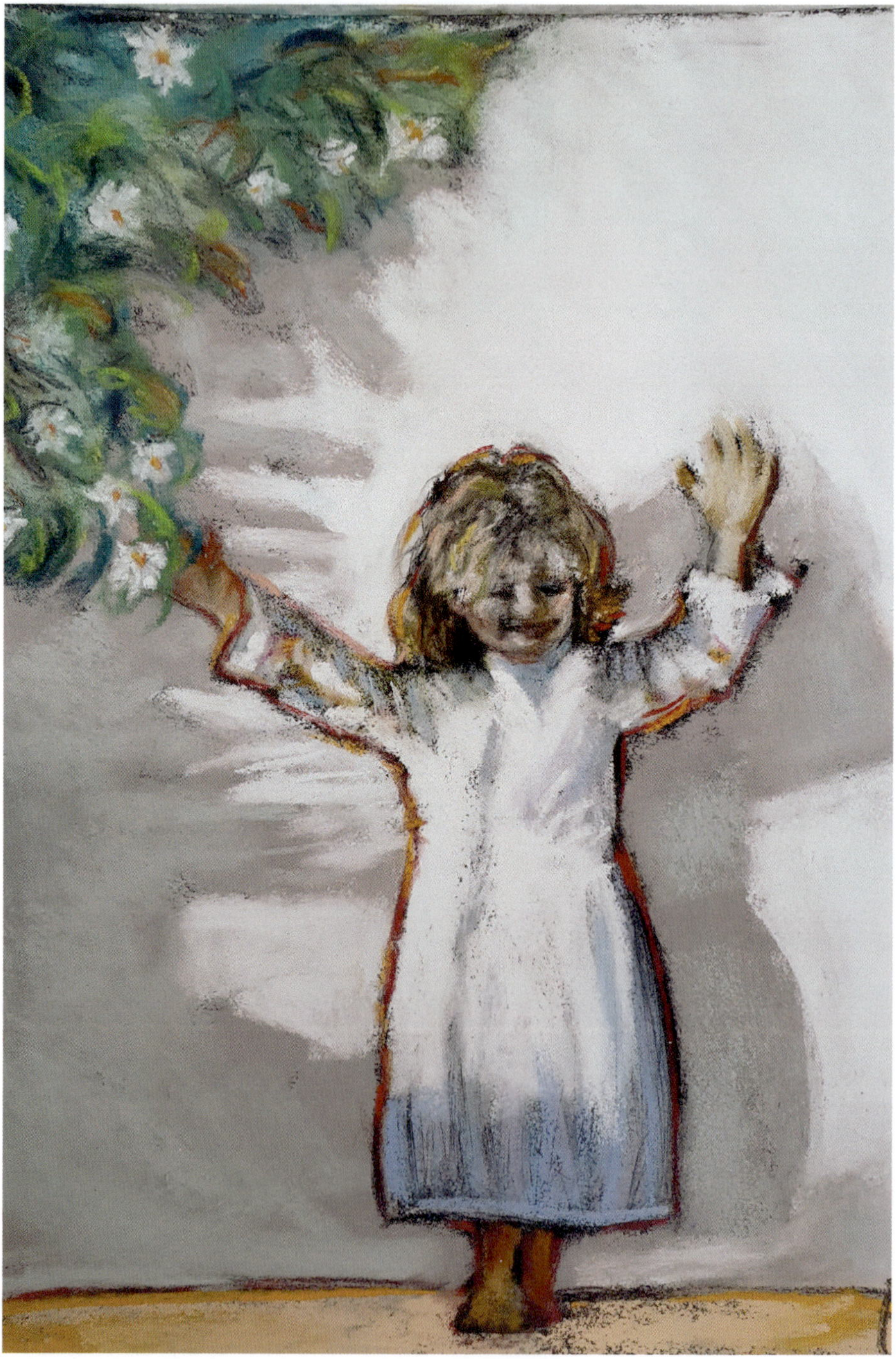

Dance with me Daddy

Dance with me, Daddy, like you did once before
the angels carried me through heaven's door.

Sing to me, Daddy, and as you hold me tight.
Remember this day is ours and let's dance all night.

I am happy in my cloud. I am free from any pain.
I can dance in the sunshine and sing in the rain.

So, dance with me, Daddy as we sing our final tune.
Let us twirl around the stars and spin under the moon.

I am tired now, Daddy, but I've had the best day
and I've left you a memory of us this way.

Forbidden Fruit

I knew that you weren't ready but I took you anyway.
The temptation was too much since I saw you on display.

Once I took a bite, I entered a world of no return.
I let desire win so I no longer felt it burn.

But as I walked away, my teeth marks in your skin,
and I felt you in my guts, I wished I hadn't let you in.

I told myself, "No more!" I had satisfied my greed.
That was just the start and forbidden became my need.

I walked past the same old tree; new fruits met the old.
The temptation wouldn't go; it felt like stealing gold.

Each time it got easier but you weren't mine to take.
I picked you out regardless, not caring about the stake.

Forbidden became my secret that I hid from all in sight.
It was also my poison that would kill me with one bite.

The Seasons keep on Changing

The seasons keep on changing.
Years are passing by,
but still the love remains
between both you and I.

Our toys are getting smaller;
blocks are now Lego,
but still the love remains,
no matter how much we grow.

Those baby cups we drank from
are nowhere to be seen,
but still the love remains,
no matter who we've been.

Our cots are now big beds.
We have rooms of our own,
but still the love remains;
in fact, like us, it's grown.

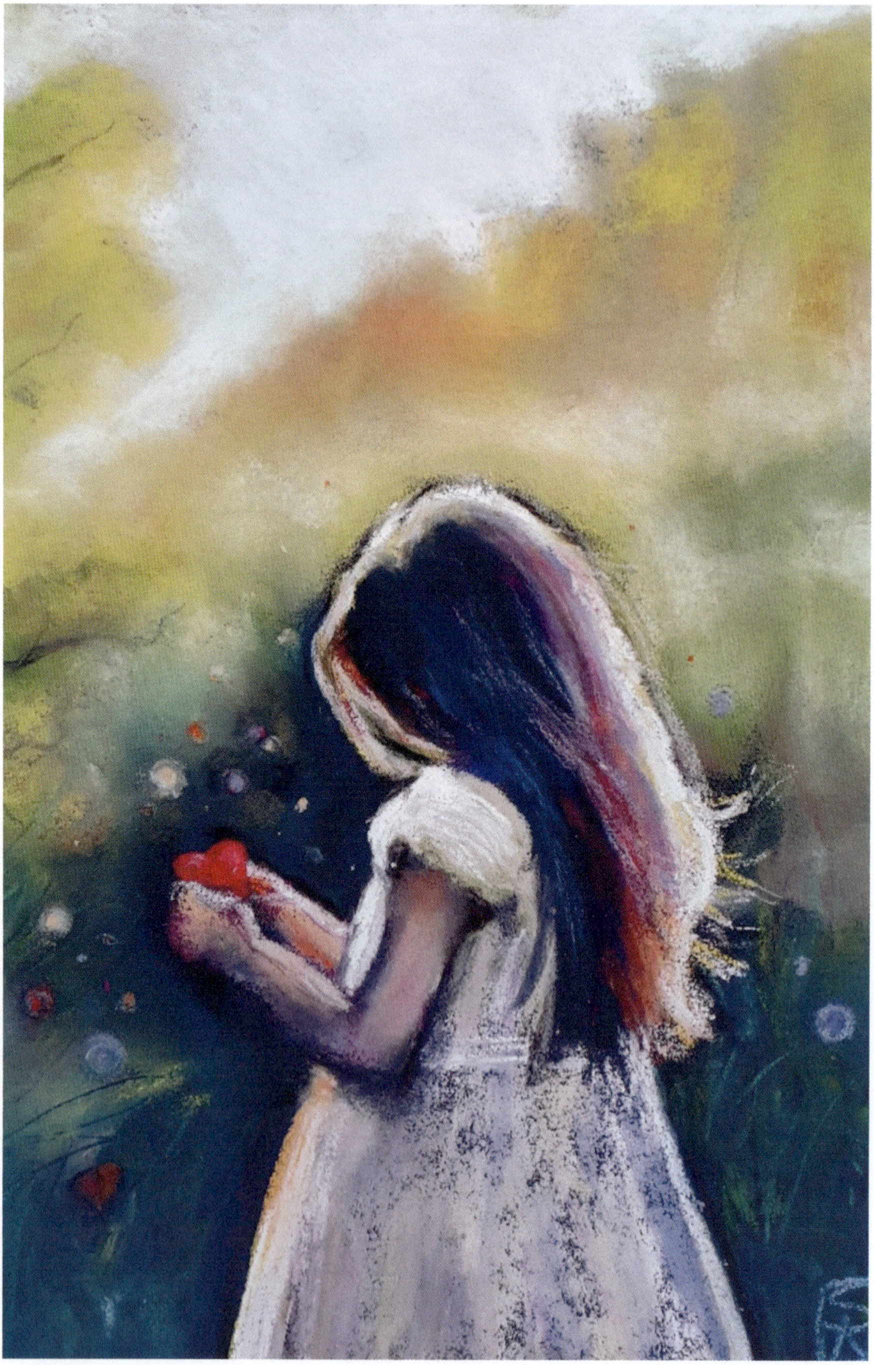

Remember Me

Remember when we spoke that night
and all you said to me
that if you had to leave this world,
you'd want me to be happy.
Remember how I shook my head and
I said, "Let's not talk this way."
You, being your wise old self, said,
"We never know when it's our last day."
Remember, as you squeezed my hand,
and told me to love again,
once more I shook my head and
said I couldn't think about the pain?
Remember how you explained
just what loving someone means?
About how knowing they are happy
is the answer to love's dreams.
Remember how you imagined,
being a tormented soul,
being lost in heaven, knowing I'm no longer whole?
Remember how you told me
not to feel guilty for moving on?
I remember smiling, as for me you were the 'one'.
Remember how I listened
as we thought it was just talk?
We didn't know the future as we enjoyed our walk.
Remember us, my darling, and all you said to me?
Replay it in your mind and stop feeling so guilty.

Another You

Grief is but a simple word, yet it has so much meaning.
It has many definitions and can make us feel demeaning.

Grief is found with loss but loss can still be seen.
It doesn't only represent someone that's once been.

Maybe someone you know with circumstantial change,
an illness taken over to now make them act strange.

The person could be yourself, each day someone new.
Yet like all kinds of grief, we still must make it through.

Grief has five letters but consumes every moment,
pulling at every emotion; just there to torment.

Grief has many branches where leaves just don't grow.
They just keep reaching out, their nakedness on show.

Grief is surrounded by colour. It stays black and white.
It represents an emptiness that's from others' sight.

Grief shall always win each battle in our mind,
so, we meet another you at each obstacle we find.

Death's Pathway

I walked along death's pathway with ghosts in my mind.
With each step I questioned what it was I hoped to find.

I looked up to the sky then down to the ground.
I looked at all the sorrow that was following me around.

I walked amongst the stories of those I had once known.
I crunched down the leaves that in my path had blown.

I listened to the whispers from the rustle of the trees.
At times I felt like giving up and falling to my knees.

The pathway still enchanting; curiosity still lived there.
The winding of the pathway still had stories yet to share.

I danced with every step and with memories I played,
and death's pathway disappeared. I was no longer afraid.

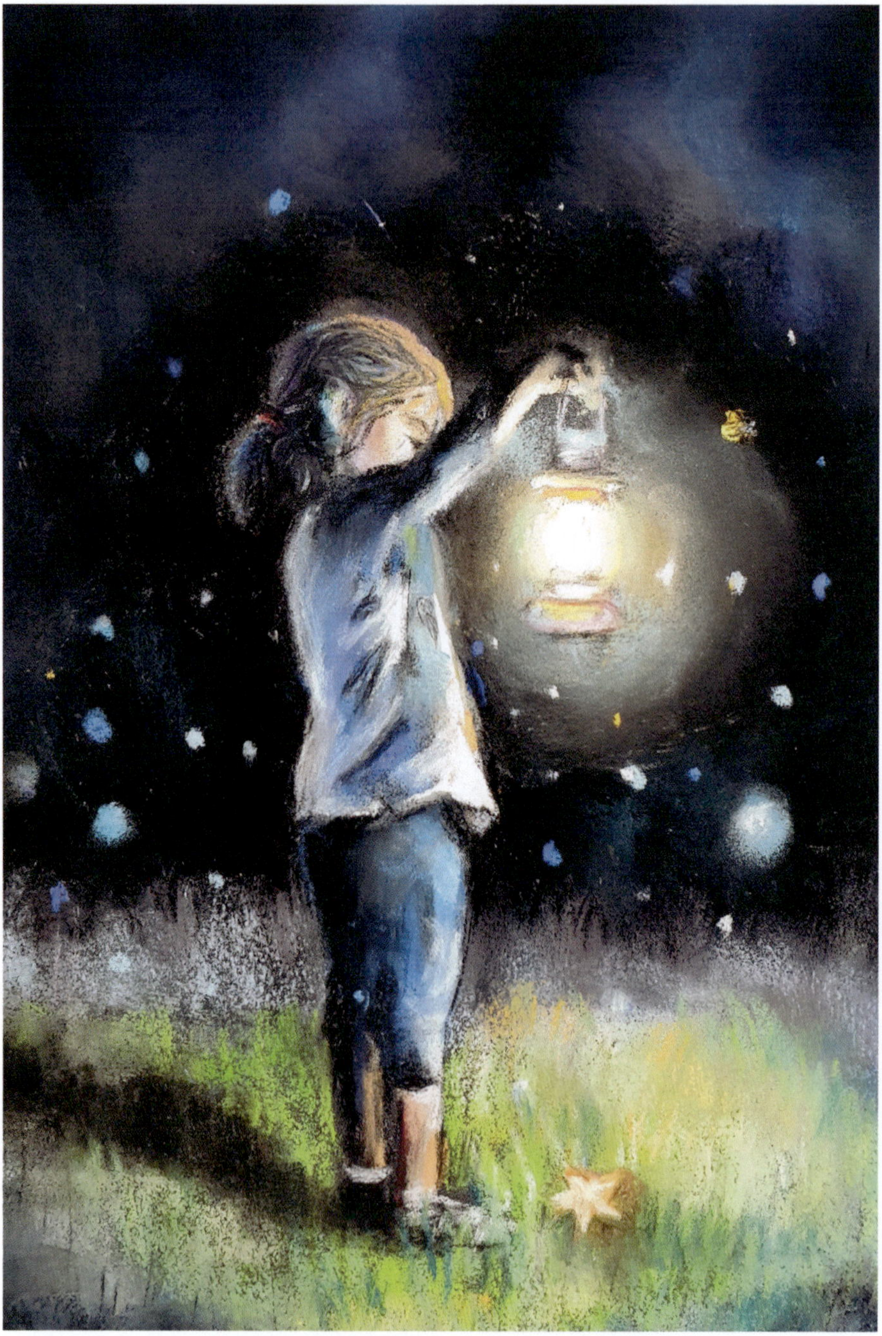

Light

Let me be the light to your darkest day.
Let me be the hope to help you on your way.

Let me be the vision of what you hope to find.
Let me be the peace needed to free your mind.

Let me be your voice until you find your own.
Let me be the love that you were never shown.

Let me take the lead whilst I am feeling strong.
Let me take your load. Let me be the one.

Let me hold the light. You have come so far.
Now let me see you shine, like the star you are.

Run Around the Block

"Let's run around the block," you said
and I thought it would be fun
but I couldn't find the block
and wondered why we'd run.

"It's raining cats and dogs," you said,
so, I quickly looked outside,
worried for the animals,
so much I stood and cried.

"Would you like a Twirl?" you asked.
I laughed and shook my head
and then I asked, "Could I
Have a chocolate bar instead?"

You spoke about the past
and all the things you done and
when you mentioned the present,
I wondered what I'd won.

You asked me to watch my sister
whilst you answered the door.
I looked on both of her wrists
but couldn't find what you asked for.

You asked if I'd like to try pickle
with my piece of ham.
I nodded and said, "Yes,"
but you brought a jar of jam.

You said the blind man was coming
to measure your windows.
This one really confused me.
How can he see where he goes?

They say I am neurodivergent
but to me I am just me,
a boy with a loving heart,
with an amazing speciality.

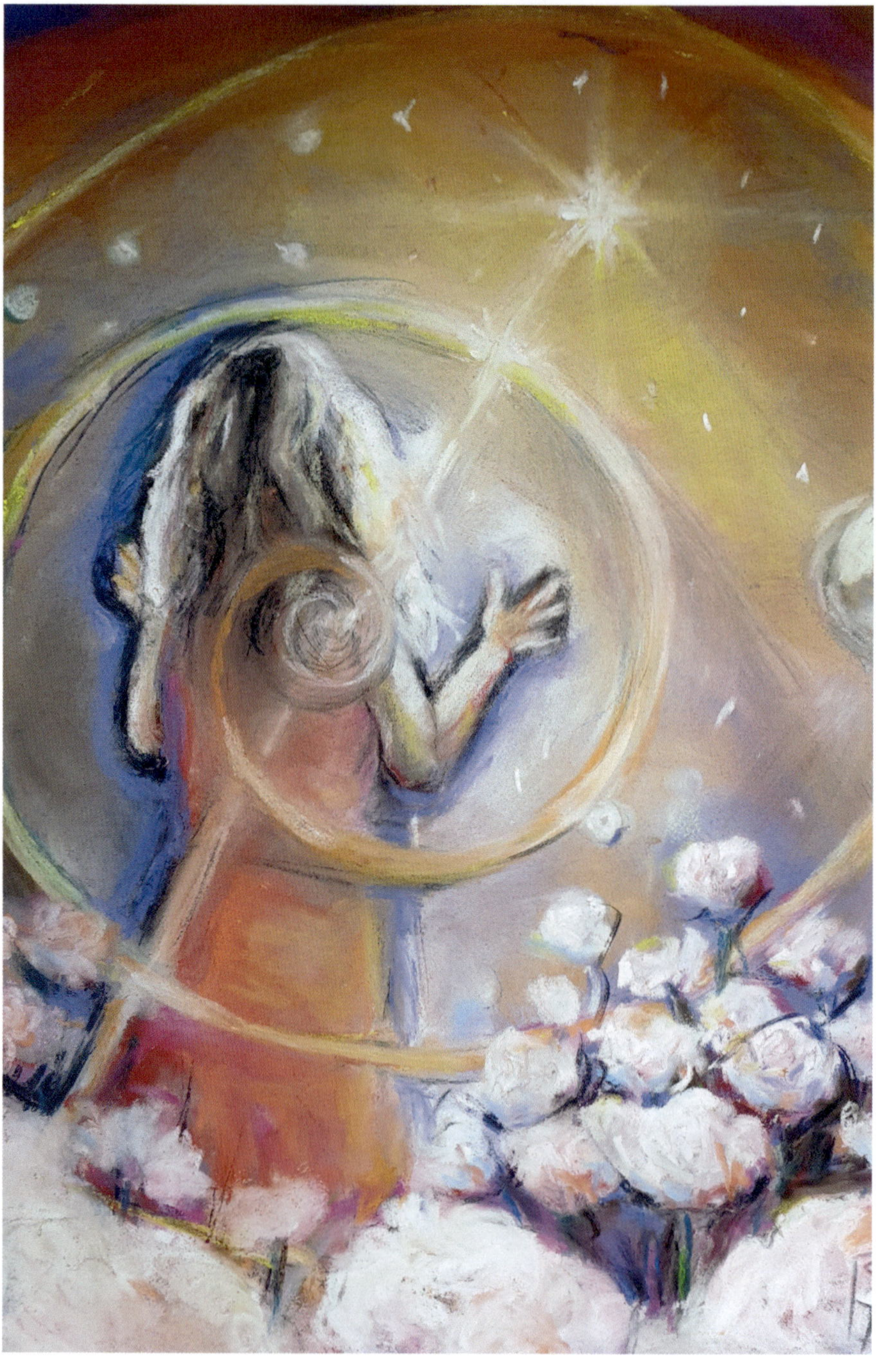

Heaven's House

I left my house a while ago but I never left my home.
It's the place my heart is rested; the place I still roam.

I now reside in heaven, along with others that I know.
I get visitors like before but now they visit with a glow.

Family often call on me, though mostly in a thought
and when they reach my door, peace is finally sought,

I'm grateful for the visit as we go down memory lane
and I never mind how many times I visit them again.

Heaven has many windows where I can see all you do.
Sometimes I close my curtains as you need privacy too.

On my birthdays I come home. I spend the day with you.
At Christmas I pull crackers just like we used to do.

On the anniversary of my passing, I sleep all day long.
That day is just for you, my love, but you only get the one.

Mothers and Daughters

I counted your fingers and then your toes,
as I bent down and kissed your cute button nose.

A mother's promise was made, as I held you tight,
that for as long as I breathed, you'd be alright.

I'd accept your decisions whilst being your guide.
I'd be the ears when you were hurting inside.

I'd be your voice when you could not speak
and be your strength when you were weak.

A mother and her daughter, an unbreakable bond;
A hidden magic like in a magician's wand.

Brought together by blood, but joined at the heart;
A mother and her daughter, friends from the start.

A Mother and her Son

A mother becomes a warrior when her son is born.
Her ball gown is replaced and armour is now worn.

No one will hurt her boy or break his heart in two.
For every other woman will have her to answer to.

A mother and her son. A warrior and her prince.
The first scent that he smelt and will remember since.

A mother and her boy, whom she will always shield.
Two hearts entwined as one through a secret sealed.

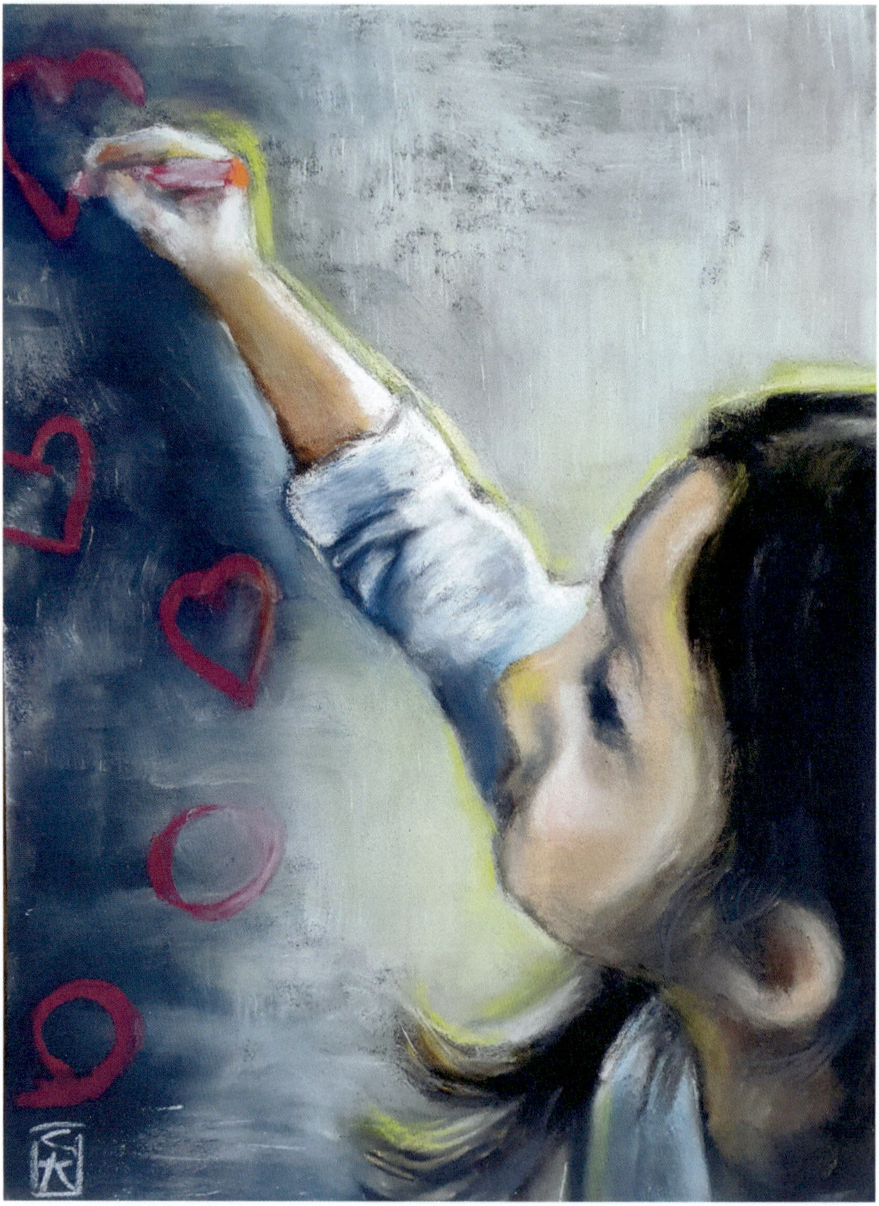

Don't Forget I Love You

With a thousand things to remember, and
so many things to do,
one thing to never forget is how much that I love you.

When your days are dark and
you think you can't get through,
one thing to never forget is how much that I love you.

When you are feeling alone and
that there's no one to talk to,
one thing to never forget is how much that I love you.

When you are looking out of the window and
don't like the view,
one thing to never forget is how much that I love you.

When you feel that no one listens and
your words become but few,
one thing to never forget is how much that I love you.

When your head tells you stories and
you wonder what is true,
one thing to never forget is how much that I love you.

When you feel close your eyes and
Before you continue,
one thing to never forget, is how much that I love you.

The End

Johnston Hale
PUBLICATIONS

If you would like to publish your own book or poetry collection, just write to us at Johnston.hale@gmail.com with your submission or visit www.johnston-hale.co.uk

Printed in Great Britain
by Amazon